Tiger Cubs

by Ruth Owen

Consultants:

Suzy Gazlay, M.A.
Recipient, Presidential Award
for Excellence in Science Teaching

Andrea Heydlauff
Managing Director
Panthera

Credits

Cover, © Eric Gevaert/Shutterstock; 4–5, © Juniors Bildarchiv/Alamy; 6, © Dave Pape/ Wikipedia (public domain); 7, © Tom and Pam Gardner/FLPA; 8–9, © Albert Visage/FLPA; 11, © Konrad Wothe/Minden Pictures/FLPA; 12–13, © M. Watson/Ardea; 14, © David Moir/ Reuters; 15, © Edwin Geisbers/Naturepl; 16, © IndexStock/Superstock; 17, © Ferrero Labat/ Ardea; 18–19, © Superstock; 20, © Dennis Donohue/Shutterstock; 21, © Jurgen & Christine Sohns/FLPA; 22T, © Nick Biemans/Shutterstock; 22C, © Joshua Haviv/Shutterstock; 22B, © Dennis Donohue/Shutterstock; 23T, Ferrero Labat/Ardea.

Publisher: Kenn Goin
Senior Editor: Lisa Wiseman
Creative Director: Spencer Brinker
Design: Alix Wood
Photo Researcher: Ruby Tuesday Books Ltd

Library of Congress Cataloging-in-Publication Data

Owen, Ruth, 1967–
  Tiger cubs / by Ruth Owen.
    p. cm. — (Wild baby animals)
  Includes bibliographical references and index.
  ISBN-13: 978-1-61772-158-8 (library binding)
  ISBN-10: 1-61772-158-1 (library binding)
  1. Siberian tiger—Infancy—Juvenile literature. I. Title.
  QL737.C23O946 2011
  599.756'139—dc22
                              2010041251

For more information, write to Bearport Publishing Company, Inc., 101 Fifth Avenue, Suite 6R, New York, New York 10003. Printed in the United States of America in North Mankato, Minnesota.

121510
10810CGC

10 9 8 7 6 5 4 3 2 1

Contents

Meet some tiger cubs

Two Siberian tiger **cubs** cuddle with their mother.

The mother tiger watches out for enemies.

She makes sure no one hurts her cubs.

Siberian tiger cub

Siberian tiger mother

All about tigers

Tigers are big wild cats.

Most tigers have orange and white fur with black stripes.

Each tiger has a different **pattern** of stripes.

Stripes

Tigers also have sharp teeth that are made for ripping and chewing food.

Sharp teeth

What is a Siberian tiger?

Siberian tigers are the biggest cats in the world.

They live in cold forests.

Their extra-thick fur keeps them warm.

Adult Siberian tiger size

Thick fur

Why are they called Siberian tigers?

Siberian tigers used to live in a large area of Russia called **Siberia**.

Today they live mainly in a small area of eastern Russia.

Where Siberian tigers live

Tiger cubs are born

When it is time to give birth, a mother tiger finds a safe place.

She hides in thick bushes and trees or among rocks.

Here, the cubs are born.

Mothers and cubs

The mother tiger feeds the cubs milk from her body.

She licks and cuddles with the cubs, too.

If an enemy finds the family's safe place, the mother carries the cubs to a new place.

What do tigers eat?

Siberian tigers eat wild pigs and deer.

The mother tiger goes hunting
by herself.

She leaves her cubs in their safe place.

She hides from her **prey** behind trees
and bushes.

16

When her prey walks by, she **pounces** and kills it!

Then she eats her meal.

Wild pig

Learning to hunt

The cubs begin to eat meat when they are about two months old.

At first, their mother brings them pieces to eat.

The cubs practice hunting by pouncing on one another and play fighting.

When they are older, the cubs go hunting with their mother.

They learn to kill prey by watching her.

The cubs grow up

The cubs leave their mother when they are about two years old.

Each one goes off to live alone.

They are good at hunting now.

They are ready to begin their grown-up lives!

21

Glossary

cubs (KUHBZ) the babies of some animals, such as tigers, lions, and bears

pattern (PAT-urn) a design that is repeated over and over

pounces (POUNSS-iz) jumps suddenly onto something

prey (PRAY) an animal that is hunted by another animal for food

Siberia (sye-BEER-ee-*uh*) a large area in Russia

Russia

border of Siberia

N
W E
S

RUSSIA

Siberia

Pacific Ocean

Index

Read more

Goldish, Meish. *Siberian Tiger: The World's Biggest Cat (More Supersized!).* New York: Bearport Publishing (2010).

Hughes, Monica. *Tiger Cub (I Love Reading).* New York: Bearport Publishing (2006).

Kalman, Bobbie. *Endangered Tigers (Earth's Endangered Animals).* New York: Crabtree (2004).

Landau, Elaine. *Big Cats: Hunters of the Night (Animals After Dark).* Berkeley Heights, NJ: Enslow (2008).

Learn more online

To learn more about Siberian tigers, visit **www.bearportpublishing.com/WildBabyAnimals**

About the author

Ruth Owen has been writing children's books for more than ten years. She lives in Cornwall, England, just minutes from the ocean. Ruth loves gardening and caring for her family of llamas.